The Struggle

Written by

Daniel A. Nagy

Contents

Dedication

To all who are lost. To all who are seeking. To the down trodden. To the meek and the weary. To those who are weak and heavy burdened. To my family, friends, and those who have ascended upon high, Lester, Don, John, and Jerry. My daughters Madelyn and Julia, and my wonderful wife Lisa.

Chapter 1: The Formative Years

Growing up on Blair Town Hall Road just south of Traverse City in the late 80's early 90's was not horrible, but maybe less than desirable. Trailers everywhere, that smell of pine trees and garbage. We were poor and my parents were both alcoholics, drug addicts and each day brought a new day of chaos. I remember sitting with a counselor and going over the past week recap and he said, "maybe you should start a sitcom." There was always some craziness going on. Fights, drunken screaming matches. My very first memory I was 5 or 6 and I was crying for water in the middle of the night. I remember my dad, drunk, stumbling down the hallway. He handed me an empty glass and I started to cry. He raged on me, picked me up and threw me across the room, and said, "go to bed!" This memory to this day in my head, is just like it was yesterday. It used to give me anxiety. Sometimes it still wakes me up at night in the form of a nightmare. I long ago forgave my dad and wish we could have had more important discussions. After my parents' divorce I saw my dad, but didn't ever really have a bond with him. We never discussed anything important and if I tried to, he would just change the subject. Luckily for me later I had a good friend Mitch and he helped me a lot with how to be a man and such.

Shortly after this memory, is my second memory I can remember that is. I was 6 ish when our trailer burned to the ground. It was midday. Gloomy. I was across the street waiting for my friend to get home. His dad was playing video games with me while we waited. He asked me to sit on the bed with him then he started to touch my private parts and began to tie me down to his bed. That's when my oldest brother Jackson came flying in, pulled me away from the guy and said the house is burning down. And he carried me home. I felt so relieved and rescued. Our trailer was almost a complete and total loss hence why I have so few pictures of me growing up. They burned.

My next memory is right after the fire. My mom drove my dad to my grandma's and dropped him off. I remember asking "where is dad going?" and my mother screamed at me "you don't have a dad any more!" I just remember crying and my brother Jackson seemed so happy. He was relieved I guess. My mom later told me my dad used to beat Jackson up pretty bad. I suppose that is then why Jackson began beating us. I never really had a good example of how to be a true man. From then on, I was always angry and frustrated, I hated God, which led to trouble and in turn led to me being involved with the court system at age 11.

So there were 5 of us total. Jackson was the oldest, then there was my brother Jody, then me, then my little sister Jasmine, and the youngest little brother Johann. It's interesting to see how things have turned out for us all and the fact that no one except Jasmine ever talks to me. I think that is coming to an end as well it seems.

Anyway, back to my story. Shortly after this we moved into the local apartments just inside the city limits of Traverse City. We were there a year or so then back to Blair Town Hall Road. Someone donated a house to my mom so we got a house, yay!

Jackson was my hero for a long time growing up, but over the years his sick and vile nature overcame him and we haven't spoken for years now.

Growing up Jackson became more and more violent and my mother came up with more and more excuses of why. I didn't care the why, I just wished I was never the one to get it, but the thing was, you never knew. We would be playing football and instead of tackling us, which hurt enough, he'd pick us up and body slam us. His older buddies did the same. I got used to the feeling of getting the wind knocked outta me. Getting beat up became so normal instead of crying I started laughing. Jackson and Jody used me for a punching bag until I became involved with the courts. But we will get to that soon enough.

I also returned some violence to Jasmine and Johann. Not as bad as what I got but more than they deserved for sure. From 6-11 I can't remember an evening I wasn't scared of my mother. My mom put my head through the wall multiple times and she's drug me down the stairs multiple times. Multiple means multiple times a month by the way. She was like a ninja with the belt. If we were real bad or she was real pissed on occasion you'd get the buckle and that really hurt. I speak on this period because so many things happened that I can't remember in what order or what time they happened. There are highlights then all this crazy crap that I remember but not exactly when.

So, when I say I was abused I'd like to explain, because abuse is pretty subjective. My mom punched, kicked, hit us with objects; the belt was most common. Now this I do not call abuse. Some of you may. It's understandable. Back then for me this is normal. The abusive stuff was evil and vile and no parent should subject their children to it! It was every kind of abuse one could think of. Stories of which I will no longer allow myself to think upon any more so for reasons of my sanity I will not get into specifics. Just know that it was scarring and I've grieved over it and have forgiven my mother of it and it never needs to be aired again. I wasn't the only one things happened to and that's all I"ll speak on that.

A thing I do remember like it was yesterday was a month after my 11th birthday. I was skate boarding in the road with a friend Kris. I went to take a pee and as I grabbed my board to run down the driveway, I heard tires squeal, a bang, and I thought nothing of it. Then my brothers come storming in and to my shock later to find out Kris got hit by a car. I was in a crying rage so angry my brothers said someone just got hit by a car they thought it was me and I told them it had to have been Kris. No one believed me though until Matt, Kris's brother, told us that night or the next morning, I do not remember. That evening changed my life forever and to this day the guilt of being a coward and running home to piss messes with me. If only I would've stayed and warned him. As tears fall as I write this, I am so sorry Kris. This was my first thoughts on 'is there something after death?'. I remember people saying to me, "he is in a better place, he is in heaven". To be honest, because I had little understanding of these things, it angered me. But this would eventually remind me of these things when I did become born again. Those who don't know about God — you can't speak to them about doctrines, they need milk, the Gospel. Saying heaven meant nothing to me.

Shortly there after was his funeral and man I didn't know what to do, to think, to say. I just cried. Seeing him in that casket, neck swollen so much it looked wider than his head. I regretted looking into that box the minute I did it. After this there was a rage in me that became out of control. I started fights just to start a fight. Anyone in authority could just go to hell. Reminds me of

John 3:19.

"[19] And this is the judgment: the light has come into the world, and people loved the darkness rather than the light because their works were evil."

There were all these grown ups running around acting like they gave a crap but really they didn't, it really started to enrage me. Teachers, school counselors, principals, all these "we are here because we care" types and then you hear them talk smack about you the minute you leave the room. I don't know how many times I stormed out of a classroom or a principal's office to stop and listen to the reaction. Now don't get me wrong, there are and were a lot of people who did care. The problem is the few who didn't ruined it for the bunch. I let my rage and fury release upon the world at that time. I went to just about every elementary school there was in the Traverse City area. Then I ended up in the "emotionally impaired" school. Short bus jokes got me into a lot of fights. My mother never really tried to solve any problem. She let the schools do as they wished, as long as it kept them from looking at her. She was so fake. The act she put on made me even angrier. I remember threatening to expose her and she said "Do it! You think you've got it bad now just wait till you're with some strangers who really don't care about you. See how fun that will be." And every time I was like, yeah she's probably right. The last straw was she was on top of me punching me and she grabbed my hair and banged my head on the floor a bunch of times. I went outside after that she locked me out told me to figure it out. I left that night and never went back. I was 11. Headed to a friends to stay the night. Stole some beer, got jumped and ended up in the hospital. My probation officer Brenda showed up, along with my grandma and my dad. Wow, it really brought out the peeps. I don't remember much about that day.

Chapter 2: Teen Angst

After getting out of the hospital, I found myself at my dad's and grandma's place for the time being. My dad had moved in with grandma after the divorce and had stayed there ever since. By this point, I was attending a "special" school for emotionally impaired kids, a place where rejects and troublemakers like me found a semblance of belonging. Traverse City, where my dad and grandma lived, became a new backdrop to my tumultuous teenage life.

I made some new friends, both at school and downtown. Not much happened apart from the occasional fights at school or downtown, and I was on auto-pilot until I turned 14. Here and there, I had probation violations and sometimes stayed at my mother's place, mainly when she wasn't around.

Then came Joe, a friend who introduced me to my first love—Patrice. When I wasn't getting high or getting into fights, this girl had me all messed up in the head. She was all I could think about. At 15, I was smoking weed regularly and did my first hit of acid. That was a trip! I remember eating it, hanging out with friends, and suddenly hearing footsteps getting closer and faster. I thought I was being jumped, so I took off running.

At some point, I stole a bike from downtown and rode it all the way to Tyler's house up in Suttons Bay, close to the Indian reservation, Peshawbestown. By the time I got there, I was full-on hallucinating and laughing hysterically at everything. We smoked some weed, and I rode down to a gas station for munchies. This was the only open gas station for about 20 miles. A tribal officer got suspicious and started asking me too many questions. As usual, I was a smart-alec. When I pulled a lighter from my pocket, my bag of weed fell out. It was like slow motion; the cop and I watched it fall. I just laughed, and he said, "Get out of my town now, and I will forget this even happened." Needless to say, I jumped on that bike and rode like I was in the Tour de France.

I made it to my grandma's by about 6am. As I sat in my room, staring at the wall, I couldn't help but think about the choices I had made. The parties, the drinking, the guys. It had all seemed so fun, so exciting, at the time. But now, as I faced the consequences of my actions, I realized that I had been living a lie.

I thought about my grandma and Brenda, and how they had always warned me about the dangers of the world. I thought about how I had ignored their advice, how I had thought I knew better. I thought about how I had let them down, and how I had let myself down.

As I sat there, feeling the weight of my mistakes, I remembered the words of the jail Chaplin Bob. He had always said that God loved me, no matter what. He had always said that God was waiting for me, with open arms, whenever I was ready to come home.

I felt a pang of guilt and regret as I thought about how I had turned my back on God. I never knew anything much of God. I had been so caught up in the thrill of the party scene, I had forgotten about the values some friends' parents and my grandma and Brenda had tried to instill in me. I had forgotten about God.

But as I sat there, feeling the emptiness and loneliness, I began to see things more clearly. I realized that I didn't have to be trapped by my mistakes. I could start over, I could make a change.

I slowly got out of bed and walked over to my desk. I opened my journal that I kept on and off and began to write. I wrote about my mistakes, I wrote about my regrets, and I wrote about my desire to start anew.

As I wrote, I felt a sense of clarity wash over me. I realized that I didn't have to be defined by my past. I could create a new future, one that was built on Christian values and faith.

I closed my journal, feeling a sense of hope that I hadn't felt in a long time. I knew it wouldn't be easy, but I was ready to take the first step towards redemption.

Unfortunately, I wasn't completely ready just yet and all I could do was get high and try to contact Patrice.

Chapter 3: Jails, Institutions, and Programs

As I looked back on those tumultuous years, I realized that I had been running from my problems instead of facing them head-on. I thought I could escape the pain and confusion through drugs and alcohol, but it only led to more suffering and chaos. The 12-step program had helped me achieve sobriety for a while, but it wasn't until I surrendered my life to God that I found true freedom.

I remember the day I hit rock bottom, feeling like I had lost everything that mattered. That's when I cried out to God, acknowledging my powerlessness over my addiction. I prayed for forgiveness and asked for His guidance. It was then that I felt a sense of peace and hope that I had never experienced before.

With God's help, I began to understand the roots of my addiction. I realized that my desire for escape and control stemmed from a deep-seated fear of not being good enough. I thought I needed to be in control of my life, but in reality, I was never in control. God was always there, waiting for me to surrender to Him.

As I delved deeper into my faith, I found that God's love and grace were the antidotes to my addiction. I learned to rely on Him instead of substances to cope with my emotions. I discovered that true freedom came from surrendering to His will, not from trying to control my circumstances.

I'm not proud of my past, but I'm grateful for the lessons I've learned. Today, I can say that I'm free from the grip of addiction, and it's all because of God's mercy and grace. I know that I'm not alone in this journey, and I'm grateful for the fellowship of believers who support and encourage me along the way.

My story is one of redemption, and I pray that it can be a testament to the power of God's love and forgiveness. No matter how dark our past may be, God can always bring light and hope into our lives.

Chapter 4: Stealing Cars

As I reflect on those reckless years, I'm reminded of the Apostle Paul's words in Romans 7:15, "I do not understand what I do. For what I want to do I do not do, but what I hate I do." I didn't understand why I kept making the same mistakes, stealing cars and lying to those I loved. It was as if I was trapped in a cycle of sin, and I didn't know how to break free.

But God was watching over me, even when I wasn't watching over myself. He saw the potential in me, even when I was stuck in my selfish desires. He saw the good in me, even when I was doing bad things.

I remember the time I stalled my mom's car in Hoosier Valley. I was so scared, but a stranger stopped and helped me out. Looking back, I realize that I could've went to jail. If he hadn't stopped to help, who knows what would have happened? Maybe I would have gotten into an accident or gotten lost in those rural roads. But God was watching over me, even in my foolishness.

And then there was the time I stole the car from the person who didn't even know her car was stolen. I didn't think about the consequences of my actions, nor did I care about the impact it would have on the owner. I only thought about myself and my own desires. But when I got caught, I told the truth, not because I was sorry, but because I was caught.

It wasn't until I surrendered my life to God that I began to understand the gravity of my actions. I realized that my selfish desires and reckless behavior were not only hurting others but also hurting myself. I began to see that my sin was not just about breaking the law, but about breaking God's heart.

As I grew in my faith, in my older years, I began to understand the concept of repentance, and regeneration. It wasn't just about saying sorry; it was about turning away from my sin and towards God. It was about making amends and seeking forgiveness from those I had hurt.

Today, I'm grateful for the lessons I learned from my past mistakes. I'm grateful for the second chances God gave me, and I'm grateful for the opportunity to make things right. I know that I'm not the same person I used to be, and it's all because of God's grace and mercy.

Chapter 5: The Patrice Era

I thought I was in love. We were both young and naive, blinded by our own desires and insecurities. Looking back, I realize it was infatuation, not love. I was willing to overlook her infidelity as long as she came back to me. I was accustomed to being with women who didn't value commitment or honesty. It was a toxic pattern, one that I didn't recognize as a reflection of my own brokenness.

We were a mismatched pair, fueled by lust and passion rather than a deep emotional connection. I stole cars and broke laws to be with her, willing to risk everything for a fleeting high. I would hitch a ride to her house, 20 miles south of Traverse City, and walk all night to get back to my place, just to be near her. It was a reckless, all-consuming obsession.

In hindsight, I'm grateful her family moved back to New Mexico. It was a blessing in disguise, saving us both from further heartache and destruction. That two-year on-again, off-again relationship taught me valuable lessons about relationships, boundaries, and my own character. I learned what I wanted and didn't want in a partner, and what I needed to work on in myself.

But I wasn't innocent in our relationship. I cheated, too. I used my fear of abandonment and low self-esteem as excuses to justify my behavior. I thought I needed to have multiple women in my life to feel secure, to avoid being alone. It was a vicious cycle, driven by my own insecurities and lack of self-worth.

It wasn't until I surrendered my life to God that I began to understand the root of my behavior. I realized that my people-pleasing and fear of abandonment stemmed from a deeper issue – a lack of faith in God's love and provision. I didn't trust that He was enough, that He could fill the void in my heart.

As I grew in my faith, in my older days, I began to see the corruption and evil in the world, including in my own heart. I learned that people's motives are often self-serving, and that true love and intimacy can only be found in a relationship with God. I began to understand that my worth and identity come from Him, not from the validation of others.

Those wild and reckless days are behind me now, and I'm grateful for the lessons learned. I'm grateful for the chance to start anew.

Chapter 6: The Downfall of the Mighty

When I was 17, I made some monumental mistakes. I was attending school on Beaver Island, but I got into trouble and decided to take a car without permission, picking up my girlfriend Patrice along the way. We headed to a friend's house in Weidman, where I knew Patrice had cheated on me with someone, but I didn't know anyone else who would join us on the run. We crashed with some friends of my buddy's for a bit, but I knew I had warrants out for my arrest. When I called my sister, she told me the cops had been looking for me and were patrolling our neighborhood.

For some reason, I thought it was a good idea to head back to Traverse City. We hung out at my mom's house until she got home, and then we took off. Little did I know, she called the police and told them I'd been there. We stopped at a car dealership near Chum's Corners and hung out until dark when we thought it was safe to leave. My buddy wanted to visit his dad in town, but about four miles from the dealership, we got pulled over. I was terrified, but I lied and told the cops I was my little brother, giving them his information. Just when I thought we'd gotten away with it, the husband of my probation officer showed up, and I knew I was caught.

It was however a huge relief to finally be off the run, to be honest. Being on the run was exhausting and stressful. I did some time in jail and was eventually released on adult probation, which wasn't much different from before, just more expensive.

From June to September of that year, I went on a crime spree that only earned me charges for Unlawful Driving Away of an Automobile (UDAA) and Use of Marijuana. I was lucky to get off with just those charges. However, my sentence was another story. The maximum sentence for one charge was 90 days, and the other was two years. Some of the other inmates, who were called "jailhouse lawyers," told me to act tough in front of the judge and I'd get the maximum sentence, but I'd be out sooner due to prison quarantine. That didn't work out so well. The judge called me some pretty terrible names, which, to be fair, were probably true. He gave me 12 months, took away my good time due to my violent behavior in jail.

I got out and went to drug treatment center that I was released from early. Ended up doing security at a local club with my probation officer's son. Ha ha. Also got a gig at a local fitness club where I began to body build.

Chapter 7: The Ego Wins

After a brief stint as a bouncer, body builder and a career in physical labor, which ended with a devastating injury, I underwent back surgery. At just 22, I transitioned my career into the addiction treatment field, and my success went to my head. I was making a ok money, but I did have frequent back problems. The constant praise from others inflated my ego. I began to believe I was the most important person in the room, deserving of honor and admiration.

My ego led me down a destructive path. I divorced my first wife and quickly moved on to my second, but that relationship also ended in failure. It was time for some introspection, so I returned to Traverse City and took a break from the chaos. I dated a girl for a short time, but I moved on.

I went back to work for a non-profit organization, using my experience to speak at schools and youth prisons. I even ran their judicial programs and was invited to speak at a school with ties to my family. That's where I met a kind-hearted teacher, and despite thinking she was out of my league, I asked for her number. We've now been married for 16 years, a story that will be told in a separate chapter.

My ego, however, continued to balloon. I was proud of my 10 years of sobriety, but I didn't always show humility. I thought I was doing people a favor by gracing them with my presence. My ego grew with each new accomplishment. I reentered the car business, starting with detailing jobs, but soon landed a sales position. I excelled, and my potential was recognized with an offer to manage finance and insurance at a large auto group in Michigan. The money was staggering, and my ego grew to match it. That's when things started to spiral out of control.

Chapter 8: Losing Control

The money was supposed to be the answer to all my problems. It was supposed to fill the gaping holes in my soul, to validate my existence, to make me feel worthy. But it didn't. It only fueled my ego, making me feel like I was invincible, like I could get away with anything. And I did. I abandoned my family, leaving behind my two precious daughters, including my baby girl who was still taking her first steps. I walked away from the people who loved me, who needed me, who depended on me. I left them to fend for themselves, to pick up the pieces of my shattered promises.

I surrounded myself with sycophants and indulgences, trying to drown out the screams of my conscience. I indulged in every whim, every fantasy, every addiction. I thought I was living the high life, but deep down, I was dying. I was suffocating under the weight of my own emptiness. The loneliness was crushing me, the despair suffocating me. I felt like I was staring into the abyss, with no safety net to catch me.

I tried to fill the void with more drugs, more women, more toys. But nothing worked. The pain only intensified; the loneliness only deepened. I felt like I was sleepwalking through life, going through the motions, but without a purpose. I was a shell of a man, a hollow husk of what I once was. The thought of suicide crept into my mind, a constant companion, a tempting escape from the agony that had become my life.

As time went by, the emptiness only grew. I felt like I was drowning in a sea of my own making. I couldn't escape the memories of my past, the pain of my childhood, the fear of being unloved, unwanted. I sought validation through the attention of women, mistaking it for love, for acceptance. But it was never enough. I was a bottomless pit, a black hole of need and desire.

I took a look in the mirror, and I saw a stranger staring back at me. A man who had lost his way, who had abandoned his family, who had abandoned himself. The struggle was real, and it was tearing me apart. I felt like I was trapped in a never-ending nightmare, with no escape, no respite. The feelings of abandonment and low self-worth had become my constant companions.

Chapter 9: Homeward Bound

My wife sent me a song. I don't know why I listened to it, but I did. It was convicting! I ended in tears and something told me to just get my things and go! Go home to Lisa and the girls! So, I packed my belongings and God led me back home to reconcile with my wife. Through the loving witness of my wife, Lisa, and my future friend, and pastor, church, friends, family (and most importantly the convicting power of the Holy Spirit) I came to realize the depth of my need for a Savior. Titus 3:5-6 says "5] he saved us, not because of works done by us in righteousness, but according to his own mercy, by the washing of regeneration and renewal of the Holy Spirit, [6] whom he poured out on us richly through Jesus Christ our Savior".

Was I too bad? Was I too far gone? It was through a simple yet profound encounter with Jesus Christ that I found the light I had been desperately seeking for so long.

As I surrendered my life to Christ, I experienced a radical transformation from the inside out! Through God's grace I then repented of my sinful nature. I grieved over my sin and began to feel I didn't deserve forgiveness. Guilt over my sin. How could a just and holy God forgive me? Through prayer and Bible study I finally saw my brokenness. Through prayer I finally felt accepted by my wife! I quit lusting over women! This wasn't done by any will power of my own! I tried so many times to feel accepted by women, and was never successful! But God. God delivered me! Through again reading the Bible and learning and understanding what God wants from us, I learned how to have a manly, healthy and most importantly a Godly relationship. Reminds me of

1 Corinthians 6:11

"[11] And such were some of you. But you were washed, you were sanctified, you were justified in the name of the Lord Jesus Christ and by the Spirit of our God."

I've learned the power and scope of what God has done for the sinner.

God crushed his one and only son as our ransom for our sin!

God helped me quit doing drugs, drinking, and smoking! Through divine intervention once again, the Lord delivered me! Glory be to God! I tried quitting all these things before and was never successful! I tried over and over again! The chains of addiction and bondage were broken at last, and I was set free to strive to live the life God wills me to live.

Through the saving grace of Jesus Christ, I found forgiveness for my sins, I saw my brokenness, I am humbled by the promise of eternal life! The gospel message is one of hope and salvation for all who believe. Matthew 11:4-6 " says [4] And Jesus answered them, "Go and tell John what you hear and see: [5] the blind receive their sight and the lame walk, lepers are cleansed and the deaf hear, and the dead are raised up, and the poor have good news preached to them. [6] And blessed is the one who is not offended by me."

Just as God reached down to rescue me from the depths of my darkness, He stands ready to do the same for each and every one of you. "For God so loved the world that He gave his only Son, that whoever believes in Him shall not perish but have eternal life." (John 3:16).

No matter how far we may have strayed or how deep our sins may be, or how much we have struggled, as I am reminded by a preacher friend of mine, in one of his ditty's you me and Jesus it says "Where sin abounds, grace does more." A reference to Romans 5:20-21

Wow... God's grace and mercy to forgive is unfathomable to me. Through the suffering of Jesus Christ, I have been reconciled to God and offered the gift of salvation. We must repent of our sins, believe in the Lord Jesus Christ, and pick up our cross and follow him.

Let us be reminded of the incredible love, grace, and mercy that God has lavished upon us. May we never lose sight of the hope we have in Christ, and may we always be ready to share what Jesus has done for us with all who are still lost. Matthew 11:28-30 "[28] Come to me, all who labor and are heavy laden, and I will give you rest. [29] Take my yoke upon you, and learn from me, for I am gentle and lowly in heart, and you will find rest for your souls. [30] For my yoke is easy, and my burden is light."

Chapter 10: Family Man

As I sit here, reflecting on the blessings in my life, my heart overflows with gratitude and love. My beautiful wife, Lisa, and I have been entrusted with two precious gifts from God - our daughters, Madelyn and Julia. These two unique and talented young ladies have brought immense joy and purpose to our lives.

Our oldest daughter is a force to be reckoned with - a natural-born leader with a keen sense of discernment and adaptability. She's street smart, confident, and has a heart that beats with compassion. And yet, she's also learning to navigate the challenges of adolescence, sometimes struggling with disrespect and impulsiveness. But through it all, we're proud of the strong, independent woman she's becoming.

Our younger daughter, on the other hand, is a shining star of wisdom and kindness. With a heart full of empathy and a mind full of curiosity, she's a true blessing to our family. She's book smart, wise beyond her years, and has a natural ability to lead others. And like her sister, she's still learning to balance her confidence with humility and respect.

Lisa and I have made it our mission to raise these two gifts from God in the ways of faith, teaching them to love and serve others, and to trust in the goodness of our Heavenly Father. We're blessed to be part of a vibrant church community that supports and encourages us every step of the way. Through thick and thin, we've committed to prioritizing our faith, our family, and our relationships with each other.

Of course, it's not always easy. Like any family, we face our share of challenges and disagreements. There are times when we struggle to see eye-to-eye, when frustration and anger get the better of us. But in those moments, we're reminded that our marriage is a work in progress, a journey of growth and learning together. And it's in those moments that we lean on God, seeking His wisdom, guidance, and peace.

As we approach our 16th wedding anniversary, I'm overwhelmed with gratitude for the gift of Lisa in my life. She's more than just my wife - she's my partner, my best friend, and my soulmate. Her selflessness, her love, and her devotion to our family are a constant source of inspiration to me. I'm a blessed man.

Today I volunteer as a musician at my church and continue to write songs and the such to bring honor and glory to God. I am a volunteer for a non profit out of Royal Oak I do minor secretarial duties and help with fund raising from time to time to again bring honor and glory to Jesus.

I also want everyone who is reading this to know and understand I am only where I am at today because of God's grace and mercy to extend to me the gift of faith. I pray that anyone reading this with a troubled soul would give in, that their heart would soften and start their journey to pick up their cross, deny themselves and follow Jesus.

Notable

Thank you to all my family and friends. Thanks to Julia and Maddie for helping me write the book.

Edited by Lisa Essenberg Nagy.

Thank you to all my family, Cheryl, Shelly and Mike, Julie and Casey, and my friends Brad and Liz, Matt and Sara, Mark and Vicki, Jerry and Mary Jo, and all you other friends and family.

Thanks to Julia and Madelyn for helping me write the book as well. Thank you to Barb for all she has done as well! Everyone needs a Barb in their life. And huge thank you to my beautiful wife Lisa.

"Glory be to God!"

Thank you to Justin and Shelly Whisler and God Alive Ministries Inc.

Made in the USA
Middletown, DE
14 October 2024

62683728R00022